St Gabriel's

The Graan Monastery
1909 - 2009

ACKNOWLEDGEMENTS

It has been a great privilege to be associated with the centenary of The Graan Monastery, and an honour to have been asked to compile this short memoir to commemorate the event. For a hundred years the Passionists at The Graan have loyally and faithfully served the people of Fermanagh and far further afield and in the process have won a special place in their affection. All our lives have been enriched by their presence among us.

I would like to take the opportunity to thank all those who helped in any way in the production of this booklet – those who took, lent or gave permission to reproduce photographs, documents or memorabilia, those who supplied information, shared their experiences and memories and those who with patience and good humour answered awkward queries and phone calls probably at inappropriate moments.

I would like in particular to thank Pat Lunny for his professional photographic expertise and those marvellous aerial shots of The Graan; likewise, Gerry Knight and Mike Breslin of *The Fermanagh Herald* for additional photographs.

Andrew O'Loughlin of Mount Argus was most helpful throughout, as were Marianna Maguire of Enniskillen Library, Mairéad and Olivia O'Dolan, Tommy McGowan, Dessie Morris and Bridie Cassidy. The staff and Religious Community at The Graan extended to me every courtesy, help and consideration. Fr Brian D'Arcy's help was invaluable as was that of Vera Toye. Patricia's cooking was superb.

The expert help and advice of Impact Printing, Ballycastle, were greatly appreciated and the final appearance of this memoir is a fitting tribute to their professionalism.

I would like to thank my wife, Kathleen, and the other members of my family for their patience and encouragement during the time I was researching and writing this memoir, and for having tolerated the disruption of domestic life to an even greater extent than normal. I thank David, Kerry and Fr Brian for taking the time and trouble to proof-read the text and I marvel at their uncanny ability to spot unerringly the missing apostrophe, the split infinitive and the dangling participle. Any inelegancies that remain are due solely to me.

Frank Rogers

Front Cover: Aerial view of The Graan taken from a helicopter by Pat Lunny

Back Cover: Detail of the Calvary at The Graan, photograph by Pat Lunny

© The Graan Monastery 2009
Printed by Impact Printing, Ballycastle
ISBN: 978-1-906689-10-0

THE GRAAN
1909 - 2009

100 Years of The Graan 1909 - 2009

1000 Years of Monastic worship

Very Rev Brian D'Arcy, CP.

Dear Father Brian,

It is a joy for me to extend warm greetings and congratulations to the community and many friends of the Passionist Fathers on the occasion of your centenary at the Graan. I am also pleased to be associated with this short memoir of Frank Rogers who, once again, has given generously of his historical expertise and writing skills to the benefit of the local Church.

The restoration, after three centuries, of organised religious life to the diocese of Clogher by the Passionists and which was shared in Fermanagh by the Sisters of Mercy and the Presentation Brothers, was a welcome sign that the long night of the Penal Laws was over. While the role of the two latter communities was specific to education, that of the Graan was quite different. It was simply to play the full spiritual role of a charismatic religious congregation in society. This role has always been supplementary to the more basic parish structure but that does not mean that it is not of primary importance. It is in fact, and has been from the earliest times, an integral and intimate part of Church life, of her holiness and mission.

How the people of Fermanagh and surrounding areas took the Passionists to their hearts is best known to the people themselves. During my own time in Enniskillen in the 1970s my colleagues and I in Darling Street always marvelled, with a frequent tinge of envy, at the enormous popularity and wide acclaim which the Fathers enjoyed. In particular, that they were available at all times for the Sacrament of Reconciliation and spiritual counselling was much appreciated and provided a haven of pardon and peace for many a troubled caller at the monastery. Without their magnetic presence Fermanagh would have been immensely deprived.

In view of the traumatic decline in vocations and religious practice which has overtaken the Church in this part of the world, it is tempting to close the book on the past. To say the least, this would be a cruel injustice to the century-old witness of the Graan. A prophetic witness of holiness may seem a tall order in a world immersed in and shaped by a surfeit of TV and consumerism. It will undoubtedly take new forms in new circumstances. But the core values, the essentials of faith and commitment, have become rooted in the soil here. With care and attention they will thrive again, as they have done in the past.

Yours, in Christ,

+ Joseph.

Bishop of Clogher

Feast of the Epiphany 2009

Congregation of the Passion

Provincial Office
St Paul's Retreat
Mount Argus
Dublin 6W
Tel (01) 4992050
Fax (01) 4992055
email: passionistprov@eircom.net

Dear Brian, Community and Friends of The Graan

On this very special occasion marking one hundred years of Passionist presence at St Gabriel's, The Graan, I want to extend to you my congratulations and best wishes.

It's difficult to imagine what life must have been like in The Graan of 1909 and the years that followed but Frank Rogers brings it alive in his wonderful account of its history. Thanks Frank.

As I read the account of how Fr Eugene and Bro Aloysius arrived at The Graan I couldn't help but admire their courage, faith and hope in stepping out into the unknown. They were following in the footsteps of St Paul of the Cross, the founder of the Passionists, and were inspired by his vision to proclaim the Word of the Cross, keeping alive the memory of the Passion of Jesus, the supreme work of God's love which he saw as the source of healing, reconciliation and peace. This vision, this message of hope is at the core of the Passionist Vocation. This treasure in earthen vessels, the lives of generations of Passionists, over the last 100 years at The Graan, bore fruit in their ministry to the many people whom they served. Thank God for his blessing upon them and upon the lives of those whom they served.

God's blessing and our gratitude to those who by their faith, support and generosity have made, and continue to make, St Gabriel's possible.

We live in changing times. The future is unknown like it was for Fr Eugene and Bro Aloysius. May God bless us too with courage, faith and hope.

In the Passion of Christ,

Pat

Fr Pat Duffy CP
Provincial

FOREWORD

The Graan Centenary

On the 25th March 2009 the Passionists and the wider community of St Gabriel's Retreat, The Graan, will celebrate 100 years. A century of service deserves a celebration. We thank God for all the Passionist priests, brothers, novices and postulants who have lived at The Graan for a long or short period. We thank God for the support we have received, and the opportunities we have been given, by the people of Fermanagh and surrounding counties. We are proud of the contribution we have made to this area and we humbly ask God's pardon for the mistakes we have made and the people we have hurt during a time of unimaginable trauma and change.

Since 1909 there have been two world wars, partition, a civil war in Ireland and almost forty years of strife, division and violence in Northern Ireland. There has also been the Second Vatican Council. Not to mention the many clerical scandals, a rise and fall in vocations, as well as changes in the practice of religion which nobody could have foreseen. Life has changed, religious life has been revolutionised. All of this has shaped the Passionists, and particularly the Community who served at The Graan.

This booklet, excellently compiled and written by Frank Rogers, could not possibly be a history of all of those events. But it is a most readable *résumé* of some important dates and events in The Graan's wonderful 100 years of life.

Frank Rogers succeeds admirably in giving us a flavour of the more significant events. It is not a history of The Graan but is rather a brief outline of how we came to be here, the extent of our ministry and an acknowledgment of the sacrifices made by so many in our 100 year history.

Frank has expertly captured the varied phases of The Graan's life highlighting, from the chronicles which were written by the Religious, some significant themes.

Nearly every family in Fermanagh has a special memory of The Graan. That goes without saying. So it would be impractical to try to capture the detailed history of The Graan in a booklet designed to be read by the busy people who visit us every day. It would be impossible to put on paper the contributions of thousands of loyal people who have kept The Graan in existence and who continue to support us to this present day.

This period in the Church's history is not a time for triumphalism but rather is an opportunity, in humility, to thank God and his wonderful people for the many graces we have all received.

A centenary is a time to look back with gratitude, to celebrate where we are at present, and to ask God's blessing on whatever future we may have together.

I want to thank all the people who sent us information and photographs and I want to thank especially those whose contributions were valued but could not be used. Most of all I want to thank Frank Rogers and his family and all who helped him in the magnificent work he has done. He has succeeded in making this brief record an interesting, accurate, honest and thoroughly enjoyable read. We have been blessed to have this gentle scholar write our story.

For Pat Lunny, the sky was the limit – literally. He hired a helicopter to ensure we got a perfect 'bird's eye view' of The Graan. I am most grateful to you, Pat, for so many excellent photographs.

I want to thank Dr Joseph Duffy, Bishop of Clogher, for his kind and generous introduction and also our Provincial, Fr Pat Duffy, CP, for his continued encouragement.

There will be many celebrations at The Graan this year, but most of them will be quiet and spiritual. The central celebration will be our Novena of Hope. It is fitting it should be so. Hope is a gift and a virtue we need more than ever at this time in our story.

We hope our celebrations, in their own sincere way, will give us a heartfelt appreciation of the privilege it has been for the Passionists of St Patrick's Province to pray and preach in the beautiful place The Graan is.

We ask the intercession of Our Lady of Hope, our founder St Paul of the Cross, our patron St Gabriel and St Charles of Mount Argus not only in the coming year but always.

Please pray for us. I can assure you that, along with the residents of The Graan Abbey Nursing Home, we Passionists here at The Graan and our devoted workers will pray for you every day of our lives.

Fr Brian D'Arcy, CP, on behalf of the Community.

THE GRAAN MONASTERY 1909 - 2009

Origins of The Graan Monastery

On Thursday, 25 March, 1909, two members of the Passionist Congregation, Fr Eugene (Nevin) and Brother Aloysius (Slattery) travelled north by train on an important mission. They reached Enniskillen at 12.40pm and after dinner in the town they walked the three miles to The Graan to take formal possession of the building which they had recently acquired from the owner, Mr Anthony Cassidy. They

Fr Eugene (Nevin), 1st Rector of The Graan

were accompanied by Mr Walter Carruth, a building contractor and father of the then Rector of Ardoyne Monastery. This was the beginning of the history of The Graan Monastery and the continuation of a monastic tradition in that part of Fermanagh that stretched back well over 1000 years.

The Monastic Tradition in Fermanagh

Today, there is only one monastery in Fermanagh – St Gabriel's Retreat, The Graan – and there are striking similarities between the modern institution and, for example, the ancient monastery of Devenish and the role played by the monks in the lives of the community both then and now.

The system of church government which St Patrick introduced into Ireland in the 5th century was the diocesan system of episcopal government, but it was found to be unsuitable for the Ireland of that time. Within a generation of the death of Patrick a new system began to take shape which soon came to overshadow the older system. The

Church in Ireland became a monastic church with abbots and monastic settlements taking the place of bishops ruling over 'tuatha' – the old tribal territories which in Patrick's time had become the basis of the Church's territorial administration. A recent survey of early Christian settlements in the Erne basin by John Cunningham has identified more than fifty monastic and early church sites. Indeed some sources would claim that the name 'Fermanagh' itself, derived from 'Fear Manaig', means 'District of the Monks'. At a time when roads in Ireland were few or non-existent the great rivers like the Erne represented the best, the easiest and the least dangerous means of transport and it was along these vital arteries that the great monastic founders built their first monasteries.

In a land without towns or villages, the monasteries of early Christian Ireland fulfilled many functions which today we would associate with urban living. Primarily, of course, the monasteries were places of prayer, but they also served as meeting places for discussing various treaties, commissions and assizes. Situated, as they often were, on the boundaries between different kingdoms they represented neutral ground where rival factions could feel safe whilst carrying on negotiations.

Devenish is hallowed ground and its sacred enclosure has been used for many centuries as a burial place. Heber MacMahon, the 'warrior bishop' of Clogher who was executed in 1650 is buried there; so also is Cuconnaught Maguire who fell at the Battle of Aughrim. In Canon JE McKenna's words, 'In these cemeteries are laid the remains of chieftains, bishops, abbots and thousands of the humbler laity.'

As the monastic system became more established in Ireland, monasteries became wealthier and their influence extended far beyond their immediate environment. This was as true of Devenish as it was of other monasteries, and the abbot of Devenish found himself presiding over vast termon lands on the west and east bank of the Erne. The area on the east bank included the area now known as 'The Graan', and the monks from Devenish, called Culdees – 'Céili Dé', 'Companions of God' – ministered to the people in much the same way as the Passionists in The Graan were to do for the next hundred years.

From about 1140 onwards the Augustinian Canons had a presence at Lisgoole Abbey and also at Rossorry, both of which would have served the Graan area. In 1583 the Franciscans took over Lisgoole Abbey from the Augustinians and remained there or nearby until well into the 18th century, ministering faithfully to the local community and commanding their affection and loyalty.

The round tower which features on The Graan logo is a replica of the round tower on Devenish Island. The tower on Devenish is one of the most attractive and popular features on the island. It is eighty-one feet high and having been carefully restored and protected over the years is one of the most perfect examples of its kind in Ireland.

On an elevated site to the south of St Mary's Priory there stands a 15th century High Cross which is unlike any other to be found elsewhere in Ireland. It is elegant and graceful with an elaborate plaited motif and a crucifixion scene in relief above the arch on the eastern face. The shape of the cross stands not merely as the instrument of Christ's punishment but in fact it is the embodiment and symbol of Christ

The Round Tower and Celtic Cross of Devenish are both represented on the right hand section of the logo. The water of the Erne is shown by the blue river flowing around the green and fertile soil of the island. Green signifies hope and life. On the left is the altar at The Graan, with its famous depiction of the Last Supper. The red tells us that Jesus gave his life to redeem us. The cross links us with Devenish and Calvary. Both Devenish and The Graan are contained within the open heart - the 'sign' or emblem of the Passionist Congregation. It is full of compassion for the suffering and, like Christ in his Passion, our calling is to journey with the lost and lonely. In our logo, too, we have an empty Cross now, to remind us that Jesus is risen. The risen Jesus is the source of all our hope. (The logo is the work of local designer, Colin Slack).

Himself. The Passionist Order was founded by St Paul of the Cross and no more fitting symbol can be found than that of the Cross itself to represent the Passionists' deep devotion to Christ's sacrifice. Taken together, the Round Tower and the High Cross on Devenish typify not only the hopes, aspirations and devotion of the Passionist Community in general, but also attest to Fermanagh's long association with monasticism and the link between The Graan Monastery of today and that older tradition of which sadly only the venerable ruins now remain.

Round Tower and High Cross on Devenish Island (Courtesy of Pat Lunny)

The Passionist Order and its Founder

The Passionist Order – more properly 'Congregation' – to which Fr Eugene and Brother Aloysius belonged was founded by St Paul of the Cross at the beginning of the 18th century. Their ministry is chiefly concerned with the preaching of parish missions and retreats, spiritual direction, chaplaincies and, increasingly, the staffing of parishes. In keeping with the high ideals of their founder, they strive to live simply in a spirit of poverty and austerity, and are distinguished by their desire and willingness to share in the problems and anxieties of the faithful to whom they minister, especially the poor and marginalised.

St Paul of the Cross was born Paolo Francesco Daneo, on 3 January 1694, in the town of Ovada, between Turin and Genoa, among the foothills of the Apennines in northern Italy. He is considered to be one of the greatest Catholic mystics of the 18th century. The son of a merchant family, Paul experienced a conversion to a life of prayer at the age of nineteen, after a conventional but pious life. His early reading convinced him that God was most easily found in the Passion of Jesus Christ which he saw as the most overwhelming sign of God's love and at the same time the door to union with Him. His life was devoted to bringing this message to all and founding a community whose members would do the same. The first name Paul received for his community was 'The Poor of Jesus'; it was only later that they became known as the Congregation of the Passion of Jesus Christ, or simply 'the Passionists'.

Sean Keating's painting of St Paul of the Cross

With the encouragement of his bishop, who clothed him in the distinctive black habit still worn by today's Passionists, Paul wrote the rule of his new community during a forty-day retreat at the end of 1720. Gradually, Paul gathered like-minded people around him, and in 1725 he received authority from Pope Benedict XIII to establish the Order of the Passionists. In 1727 he was ordained to the priesthood and ten years later the first Retreat – the name Passionists traditionally give to their monasteries – was opened on Monte Argentario, with a community of just nine members.

After a long life of exemplary piety, austerity and devotion to the poor and the deprived, Paul died on 18 October 1775, at the Retreat of Saints John and Paul in Rome. By the time of his death, the Congregation founded by him had 180 Fathers and Brothers, living in twelve Retreats, mostly in the Papal States. There was also a monastery of contemplative sisters in Corneto (today known as Tarquinia), founded by Paul a few years before his death to promote the memory of the Passion of Jesus by their life of prayer and penance. St Paul of the Cross was beatified on 1 October 1852, and canonised on 29 June 1867 by Blessed Pius IX. Friend of kings, confidant of popes, tireless advocate of the poor and outcast, Paul exhibited to a heroic degree those virtues of a Christian life that ensured that his memory would be revered not just by his devoted followers but by all those who strive to follow the precepts of Christ. His feast day is now celebrated on 19 October.

The Passionists in Ireland and the Province of St Patrick

The Passionists came to Ireland in 1856, founding their first Retreat at Mount Argus in Dublin. In 1868 they came to Ardoyne and subsequently founded houses at Crossgar in Co Down, Collooney in Co Sligo and other less permanent foundations. Some famous Passionists have been Fr Paul Mary Pakenham, nephew of the Duke of Wellington and first Rector of Mount Argus, Fr Ignatius Spencer, great-uncle of Winston Churchill and great-great-great-uncle of Princess Diana, Bishop St Vincent Strambi, Blessed Dominic Barberi, who established the first Passionist residence in England and received the famous John Henry Newman into the Catholic Church, and the recently canonised St Charles of Mount Argus; St Maria Goretti is also venerated as a Passionist because her spiritual formation had been guided by them and she had yearned to be a Passionist nun. It was a Passionist priest, Fr Cuthbert Dunne, attached to St Joseph's Church, Paris, who ministered to Oscar Wilde on his deathbed.

The Townland of Graan

The townland of Graan is at the south-eastern tip of the Catholic parish of Botha, formerly called Devenish East but now more commonly known as Derrygonnelly. The parish is one of the largest in area in the Diocese of Clogher. Its population has declined from 12,700 in 1841 to 8,500 in 1851, 3,011 in 1993 and 2,791 in 2000. Sixty percent of the population is Catholic. The word 'Graan' seems to be derived from the Irish word meaning 'gravel'. In ancient records it was written as 'Finngran', from the Irish *'Fionn-ghrean'* meaning 'white gravel'. Significantly there are several limestone quarries in the region today and of course when ground down the limestone would produce a whitish gravel. Another meaning of 'Graan' is 'Grove of the trees', which would also be appropriate to The Graan in its sylvan setting.

The names of the successive proprietors in the Graan area from the 17th century onwards reflect the new order that had come to Fermanagh in the wake of the Ulster Plantation – Davis, Hastings, Wallace, Archdale. In the aftermath of the 1641 Rebellion, a certain William Hamilton was made Cromwellian Commissioner of Revenue and he lived at Graan. In the 1788 Roll of Electors, Baptist, Samuel, George and David Gamble are listed as residing at Graan. Ten years later, at the time of the United Irishmen Rebellion, one of the principal recruiting agents for the organisation was William Gamble, who escaped many attempts to capture him. Gamble lived at Graan.

In a publication by A. Atkinson in 1833 there is a revealing account of Graan House. It reads:

Graan House is a respectable feature of the Fermanagh estate of General Archdale, and is the seat of Adam Nixon, Esq., clerk of the peace for the County of Fermanagh. It stands on a proudly elevated lawn of thirty-four Irish acres, apparently well cultivated and embellished with useful and ornamental trees. It commands a pleasant prospect of Castle Coole (the seat of the Earl of Belmore) and of Portora and also a glimpse of that Lough which is the glory of Fermanagh, and which – though the spot that is seen is but as a speck in the ocean – communicates a ray of brightness to this little scene.

Graan House constitutes an interesting retreat from the noise and bustle of Enniskillen … The comfortable and well circumstanced retreat may be regarded as a pretty fair specimen of the numerous respectable homesteads of the yeomen of Fermanagh, that are scattered over the face of all the principal estates in that county. It is distant from Enniskillen, which is the post town to it, about two [sic] miles.

The 1901 census shows three families living in Graan townland – the Cassidys, the Glenns and the Brackens. Anthony Cassidy, the head of the Cassidy family, had by this stage acquired The Graan and he resided there with Jane Cassidy, his wife, and a son, Henry. They had three servants – Catherine Green, a cook and domestic servant, Margaret Love, a general servant, and James Cassidy, a farm servant, who was probably a relative of Anthony, as he also hailed from Co Cavan. Clearly, Graan House was an extensive property in an agricultural setting with cattle and horses playing a significant role in the economy. Neither sheep nor pigs seem to have been kept, nor, surprisingly, was there a potato store on the farm. It was predominantly an economy based on cattle rearing and grazing, with some tillage.

A LATER VIEW OF OLD HOUSE.

The Passionists Take Possession of The Graan

In 1909 the Passionist Communities in Ireland belonged to the Anglo-Hibernian Province of St Joseph which embraced not only Ireland but England, Wales and Scotland as well. The novitiate, where young Passionists were trained, was at Broadway in Worcestershire in England but most of the candidates for the Order came from Ireland. Consequently it was felt desirable that a novitiate would be established in Ireland nearer to the source of vocations, which would also serve as a base for organising parish missions and retreats. It was against this background that The Graan Monastery was founded in 1909.

In fact the decision to move the novitiate to Ireland had been taken at the Provincial Chapter in July 1908. It was a good time to buy, and the Passionists, ever alive to the opportunity of securing suitable premises, kept a close eye on the market. Their choice eventually settled on Anketel House, an imposing mansion set in 132 acres of land four miles from Monaghan town in the Diocese of Clogher. The Bishop, Dr Owens, a personal friend of Father Malachy, the Provincial in England, gave his permission for the establishment of a house of the Order in his diocese, but the proposed deal to purchase Anketel House fell through.

The Passionists then cast around for some other place in the diocese for their novitiate. They soon became aware that Graan House was for sale and that it would admirably suit their purposes. The premises were inspected on 2 February 1909 and the property, stock and outdoor effects were purchased on 5 February. The following day, Dr Owens, welcoming the Religious of the Congregation of the Cross and Passion to his diocese, gave his approval in writing, sanctioning the foundation of a Passionist Retreat at The Graan, Enniskillen, and commending the Congregation to the charity and goodwill of his priests and people.

What factors influenced the Passionists in the choice of The Graan as a suitable place for their Retreat? Firstly, was its availability, but secondly was the consideration that the Bishop of Clogher had already given oral permission for the establishment of an institution in his diocese and had heartily welcomed the Passionists.

There were other reasons which led to the Passionists settling in The Graan. As we have seen from the 1901 census the premises were large and the house in a reasonably good state of repair. Broadway was too distant and neither Mount Argus nor Holy Cross, Ardoyne, could accommodate the numbers of young men joining the Order. The Graan had many attractions: from a practical point of view, it was within relatively easy reach of Dublin and Belfast, both of which cities were connected by a three-hour train journey to Enniskillen; from there it was about an hour's walk to The Graan; it lay in the heart of the beautiful Fermanagh countryside, nestling in the midst of rolling hills, broad meadows and stately trees. There is an air of languid peace and serenity at The Graan, making it an ideal setting where young men could quietly pursue their course of study, prayer, reflection and contemplation of the Passion and Death of Christ.

The Graan and the Cassidys

Probably the deciding factor influencing the Passionists' choice of The Graan was that they knew the owner and he was well disposed towards them. The owner was Mr Anthony Cassidy, a successful and prominent businessman, then retired and living in Dublin. He was born at Corrahoash, near Dowra in Co Cavan, and as a young man he had been apprenticed as a shop-boy in an establishment at Fairview, Belmore Street, Enniskillen. He worked hard, soon becoming manager, eventually purchasing the business. He went on to own the Bond Store at Market Street where whiskey and tobacco were stored, another store at Paget Square and an establishment in High Street where McHenry's chemist shop was more recently situated.

Anthony Cassidy

Anthony Cassidy's son, Maurice, emigrated to Argentina, but he became ill there and died in Buenos Aires shortly afterwards. During his illness he was attended by a Passionist Father, Fr Vincent (Logan), who administered to him the Last Rites. Before he died, Maurice had asked Fr Logan to contact his parents and reassure them that he died faithful to his old religion. Fr Logan did as he had been asked, visiting Anthony Cassidy and his wife who then lived in Dublin. They were forever grateful to Fr Vincent and the Passionists for everything they had done for their beloved son.

Anthony Cassidy had bought The Graan in the year 1881 from a man called Keane, who had bought it some three years earlier from the Nixon family. The Nixons still owned a small portion of the property but they were bought out by Cassidy for the sum of £170. Keane was paid £2,400 for his share.

Mr Cassidy retired from business about 1900. His son, Henry (Harry), then took over the running of the farm at The Graan but he was tragically killed in an accident at Clones Railway Station. After his death, The Graan was rented on a monthly tenancy basis to different people successively, mainly officers of local British regiments. Major Pierce of the 27th Inniskilling Fusiliers occupied it for a time, and by a strange coincidence, at the time of its purchase by the Passionists, the tenant was a Mr Pakenham, who bore the same name as the illustrious first Rector of Mount Argus.

Sr Mary Malachy (O'Dolan) in a letter to her sister-in-law, Lizzie, 1965, relates the following little anecdote:

It seems that Uncle Anthony, a Passionist (perhaps the Provincial) and a valuator came to the Graan one day. When everything was valued they finished up in the stables where there had been a heap of old horse shoes. Uncle said put a value on them! then turning to the Passionist (perhaps handing him the title deeds, said "I give it to God and to you". [sic]

Anthony Cassidy had carried out considerable improvements to the house and lands at The Graan since he had acquired them in 1881. It is an indication of his goodwill to the Passionists that, for all he was a hard-headed businessman, he agreed to sell the house and land for the same price he had bought it for many years before. He went even further and consented to return £500 to the Order on the understanding that a mural tablet would be erected in the new church in memory of his son, Henry, who had died so tragically two years previously. When he died in 1910, Anthony Cassidy left a substantial sum of money to the Passionists on condition that they would offer up Masses for his soul.

Mairéad and Olivia O'Dolan, grand-nieces of Anthony Cassidy, live at Belcoo and kindly supplied much of the above information.

PRAY FOR THE GOOD ESTATE OF
ANTHONY CASSIDY AND JANE HIS WIFE
FORMER OWNERS OF THE GRAAN
GENEROUS BENEFACTORS OF THIS RETREAT
IN MEMORY OF THEIR BELOVED SON
HARRY CASSIDY

The Graan in 1909

Though structurally sound, the building the Passionists came to was in a rather neglected state. The roof and the interior walls were tolerable, but the yard and out offices were in a rather unsanitary condition. The part of the building which was to become the church was made up of stables and a coach-house and the remaining part of the room, soon to become that of the Master of the Novices, was all byre.

To add to their troubles the building which the Passionists came to occupy was said to be haunted – by, of all people, the late Captain Sandy Nixon, a staunch Orangeman who had formerly lived there and who was said to have had an Orange hall in that part of the 1909 novitiate immediately beside the sacristy. It is unlikely that the Passionists lost much sleep over the reported apparitions, being more concerned about the *Holy* Spirit than the variety said to roam the halls of The Graan. At any rate, not everybody held the late Captain in poor regard, for as one old Catholic man put it with typical Fermanagh magnanimity: 'If you were in a howldt, he was just the one to get you out of it.'

Sean Keating's painting of St Gabriel

St Gabriel

Immediately upon the Passionists' arrival at The Graan the picture of Blessed – now Saint – Gabriel was hung in the room to the right of the entrance, later to become the refectory. St Gabriel was a brilliant young Italian Passionist student, known in the world as Francis Possenti, son of a professional and respected family. He grew up in a household where devotion to Our Lady of Sorrows was a hallmark of family life. He lived the life of a typical teenager, dancing, hunting, going out with girls, but he still felt something was lacking. He turned to Jesus and His Sorrowful Mother and felt an inner calling from Our Lady to become a Passionist. This he did after many trials. As a Passionist his love grew daily for Our Lord and Mary, the Virgin of Sorrows, and he soon came to the perfection of Christian virtue. He died from tuberculosis at the young age of 24. St Gabriel was declared a Saint by His Holiness Benedict XV in 1920. He is patron of young people, students, seminarians, clerics, Italian youth and of the region of Abruzzi in Italy. His feast day is celebrated on 27 February. In his exemplary lifestyle, devotion to Our Lady and pursuit of academic excellence he was regarded as an outstanding example for Catholic youth of Christian virtue and devotion to the Passionist ideal.

First Church at The Graan

An old bell was discovered in a passageway and the morning after their arrival Fr Nevin celebrated the first Mass in the new Retreat. The Passionists had arrived in The Graan.

Early Years at The Graan

The Passionists at The Graan had to overcome many difficulties in the early days of their existence, including a protracted dispute over a right-of-way to their new foundation, but the people of Enniskillen and the surrounding countryside were delighted at their coming. Mrs Hanahan of Silverhill was the first to welcome them by letter and the first visit of welcome was paid by Mr Francis Duffy of Belmore Street. It was the beginning of a long and intimate relationship between the people of Enniskillen and Fermanagh and the Passionists who had come to settle in their midst and serve them loyally and faithfully over the next 100 years.

They were also heartened by a message relayed through Fr Joseph, a senior member of the Passionist Community in Rome, conveying the good wishes and blessing of Pope Pius X to the new foundation at The Graan. Fr Joseph had had an audience with the Pope and found him interested and well disposed to the new venture. He had sent his blessing to all those who would by word or deed contribute to The Graan's success. Gradually the Passionists began to

First Church at The Graan, 1915

establish themselves in the community. The little church, formerly a stable, was quietly opened to the public on 25 July, exactly four months after the Passionists had taken possession of The Graan; evening devotions with Benediction were held on Sundays, Wednesdays and Fridays. Writing somewhat later, Michael Flanagan, of Devenish, relates how up to thirty people used to walk from Enniskillen on a Sunday evening to attend Benediction at The Graan – 'That was our pastime for the day'. The first public or outdoor procession at The Graan took place on 4 July 1915, to a new Calvary which had recently been erected in the grounds.

Church and Old Novitiate, 1915

Expansion and Growth

The Graan was prospering, and with the ever-increasing number of novices the decision was taken to build a new, bigger and better novitiate to

Fr William (Brennan)

accommodate the growing influx. On 31 October 1917, the foundation stone of the new Retreat was laid by Fr William, who was then Rector. Formal possession of the new building was not taken until 13 November 1920.

Passionist Novitiate, St Gabriel's Retreat, before 1937

The Graan Retreat in the 1920s

Reception Committee, The Graan, 1926

A New Church

The little church which had served the Community at The Graan, and the people who came to worship there, was proving too small for the purpose, and the decision was taken to build a new one. The foundation stone was laid on 9 May 1925. John and Michael Donnelly were the main contractors, and the entire enterprise had been made feasible through the generosity of Mr Moore and his wife, a native of Enniskillen, then living in Phoenix, Arizona. Work on the new church progressed rapidly and it was dedicated by the Bishop of Clogher, Most Revd Dr McKenna, assisted by Archdeacon Tierney, PP, VG, Enniskillen, on Pentecost Sunday, 23 May 1926. The total cost of the building was £33,000.

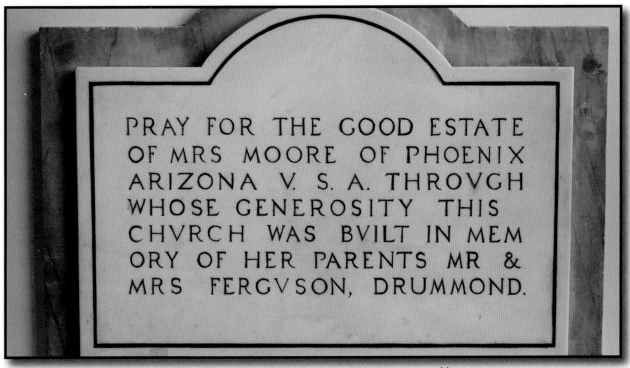

Plaque in The Graan commemorating Mrs Moore and her parents

Dr McKenna at dedication of new church, 23 May 1926

Interior of Church of St Gabriel

Front view of Church of St Gabriel and Novitiate, before extension

Province of St Patrick

The growing importance of Mount Argus, The Graan and Holy Cross, Ardoyne, in the Passionist Congregation was recognised in 1927 when a new province of St Patrick was created. It embraced the foundations in Ireland and St Mungo's, Glasgow. From 1952 onwards, Overseas Missions were founded in Africa – in Botswana, South Africa and Zambia. The province also created a presence in Paraguay, South America. In Ireland and Scotland, Passionist Preachers were in high demand for parish missions and for retreats to priests, religious and laity.

Many of these itinerant preachers were assigned to The Graan and were frequently absent from the monastery for long periods.

A New Calvary and Lourdes Grotto

On 21 September 1930 a recently erected Calvary was solemnly opened and blessed, and 4 October of the following year saw the solemn opening of the new Lourdes Grotto, built by voluntary labour. It was attended by an estimated crowd of 10,000 with General Eoin O'Duffy, Chief Commissioner of the Gardaí Síochána, and other distinguished guests among those who were present.

Fr Ignatius, General Eoin O'Duffy and distinguished guests at opening of Lourdes Grotto

Novitiate Extended

espite the improvements indicated above, the increasing number of students made it necessary to extend The Graan by the addition of a third storey, thus altering its appearance from what one writer described as being like a French Foreign Legion outpost in a PC Wren novel. The new novitiate was formally opened on 26 July 1937. The main contractors were J Donnelly and Sons, Enniskillen, and the total cost of the new extension was £8,600.

Completing the third storey

The monastery, with the new third storey housing the Novitiate

The Graan and World War II

The early years of the Second World War receive scarcely a mention in the annals of The Graan. A special altar in honour of Our Lady Queen of Peace was put up on the Sanctuary and remained there throughout the month of May 1941. A bus outing for the whole Community had to be cancelled due to petrol rationing. There was more excitement over the purchase of a new tractor, a concert in Enniskillen Town Hall in aid of The Graan Debt Reduction Fund, the appointment of Dr O'Callaghan as Bishop of Clogher, the annual hay harvest and the completion of a new garden named 'Our Lady's Bower' than there was over Rommel's campaign in North Africa or the general progress of the European War. Sadly, this state of affairs at The Graan did not continue and the war came to its door with a vengeance in 1943.

On 9 December 1943, Dr Eugene O'Callaghan, the recently appointed Bishop of Clogher, was paying an historic visit to The Graan. As Joe O'Loughlin graphically describes, the bishop and his hosts were having lunch in the parlour when they became aware of an aeroplane behaving erratically in the vicinity of the building. It was seen to circle several times over the monastery and then swoop low over the valley by the lawn field. To their consternation it seemed at one stage to be making directly for The Graan. The pilot managed to swerve and climb at the last minute but then seemed to lose control and the plane plummeted earthwards. The right wing struck a tree in the Folly Field and breaking off, became lodged there; the main body of the plane then somersaulted and careened fifty yards along the ground before another tree brought it to a shuddering halt. The plane immediately burst into flames.

The monks who had witnessed the scene rushed from The Graan and used fire extinguishers to quench the flames. Survivors were pulled from the wreckage. Fathers Eugene, Declan, Fergus and Oliver ministered to the dead, the dying and the injured; others brought blankets. Some, finding their sandals a hindrance, threw them away and worked in the muddy field in their bare feet. All rendered whatever assistance they could.

Seven American airmen perished in the aircraft but the terrible event led to the forging of a close and long-lasting friendship between the Passionists at The Graan and the American forces stationed in Fermanagh at Ely Lodge, Castle Archdale and St Angelo. Mainly through the good offices of Fr Cyprian, OFM, Chaplain to the Catholics of the 13th Infantry of the 8th Division of the US Army, Fr Sylvius from The Graan was invited to preach to the troops at Midnight Mass in the grounds of Ely

Lodge. Practically every Sunday evening thereafter a truck load of 'Yanks' arrived at The Graan for Devotions. A special High Mass was arranged for them and 28 lorries brought 600 soldiers to The Graan where the American flag was flown. On 'Mother's Day', the second Sunday of May, 700 US troops attended a solemn High Mass in 'Our Lady's Bower'. The troops on that occasion contributed £250 which was used for the erection of a white marble statue for the bower.

The American Memorial

The Developing Years

Fr Tom Maguire of Newtownbutler was proving a good friend to The Graan and it was in his parish that the Passionists from The Graan gave their first mission in the diocese on 4–11 June, 1944. Another good friend was Fr McCaffrey of Derrygonnelly who organised a concert in the Hibernian Hall in Boho, presenting the proceeds to The Graan. Concerts were also held from 1940 onwards in the Townhall, Enniskillen, with a Belfast Dramatic Society called 'The Super-optimists' being the main performers; the chief organisers were Bert Warren, Paddy Hunt, Eddie Kilpatrick and Brother Bede.

Tragedy came to the little Community at The Graan on 19 June 1945 when a novice, Confrater Ferdinand (Aloysius Daly, right), drowned while bathing in Lough Erne. He was just twenty-two years of age and had worked for two and a half years as a civil servant before joining the Passionist Order. He was a native of Belfast.

The late '40s and early '50s saw the death of many who had been associated with The Graan since its foundation in 1909. Fr Malachy (Gavin), who had shown such zeal in establishing St Gabriel's Retreat, died on 30 April 1948. Fr Eustace (McAuley), a native of Garrison, died on

15 February 1951 and Fr Terence (Barrett), a former Rector of The Graan, died on 15 August of the same year. The much-loved Fr Ignatius (Gibney) passed to his eternal reward on 15 September 1952 and Fr Ephrem (O'Connell), one time Master of Novices, died on 17 June 1953. James Murray, a farm worker and faithful servant of The Graan for twenty-five years, departed this mortal coil on November 1947, and Margaret Boyle, for many years the organist in The Graan, died on 12 December 1948.

Fr Ignatius Gibney

Fr Ignatius Gibney, one of Ireland's best-known and loved Passionists, is remembered in Fermanagh with great affection. He was born in Dublin in 1889, ordained in 1913 and appointed to The Graan in 1927. For years he ministered there bringing healing and reconciliation to the crowds who came to him with their troubles. It was the sick in particular who claimed his unreserved affection, but he was also renowned as an outstanding preacher. Despite his oratorical skills he remained a man of unspoilt simplicity and humility. On the day of the Irish delegation's departure for peace talks in London following the War of Independence, he heard the confession of Michael Collins. He died in a Dublin nursing home on the Feast of Our Lady of Sorrows and is buried at Mount Argus.

Fr Ignatius Gibney

A whole generation of loyal friends and devoted servants at St Gabriel's – and only some are mentioned here – had passed away and the Community was poorer for their passing. There were, however, men and women of equal calibre ready and willing to take up the challenge and guarantee the future success of The Graan. Jack Keenan became choir master and Miss Lunny organist, and two newly ordained priests, Fr Marius (Donnelly) of Enniskillen and Fr Salvian (Maguire) of Florencecourt were welcomed to St Gabriel's in 1952. At the Christmas services that year St Michael's Old Boys' Choir sang at the Masses. The entire Community numbered twenty-eight. Fr Alphonsus was Rector.

Graan Choir and Altar Boys, 1958, with Traveller children in front row

The Graan Choir, 1960-61, pictured with Bishop Urban Murphy

Missionary Outreach

Just as the monks of ancient Ireland, Colmcille, Columbanus and Gall, were ever anxious to spread the faith abroad, the Passionists, too, were keenly aware of their overseas responsibilities. Many of those who started their training for Passionist life in The Graan were later to work in Tanganyika, Botswana, South Africa, Zambia and Paraguay. From The Graan in 1946 Fr Fergus joined Frs Theodore, Vivian and Matthew to work in Tanganyika. Many from the locality who became Passionists spent long periods overseas, including Frs Jerome, Salvian, Cosmas, Sylvius and Arthur McCann. Frs Finian Harte and Dermot P Cleary were renowned for their fund-raising for the overseas missions.

The Graan Farm

The Passionist Community at The Graan was very much dependent on the farm produce for their day-to-day needs. It was always a struggle to get the hay saved and when there was a wet season the potato crop also suffered. Such a season occurred in 1954, and so many people lost their potato crop in floods that year that it was reported that one man ate a whole acre of potatoes for his dinner. The farmyard was renovated in 1955, a new silo unit installed, calves and cattle-sheds and a pig-parlour built and a new carpark

provided at the same time. The work was made possible largely through the generosity of Mrs Conor McManus of Silverhill, Mr McGowan of the nearby quarry, John Dooris, Francis Bradley, John James Scallon and many other willing hands. In those days before myxomatosis, rabbits were a problem around the farm. The Rector purchased a double-barrelled shotgun, but there is no record of his ever having shot anything.

Fund-Raising

Dependent as it was on voluntary contributions, fund-raising to meet its many requirements was always a problem for the Community at The Graan. Recognising their difficulty, men's and ladies' committees were formed to assist in the work. The Graan has always been innovative and imaginative in its endeavours to augment its coffers, but surely never more so than in 1956 when a raffle was organised for which the first prize was a trip to Lourdes, second prize the winner's weight in coppers and third prize the winner's height in pound notes. No doubt a few private prayers were whispered that the second prize winner might not be the man who ate the acre of spuds for his dinner in 1954 and that the third-prize winner would not resemble a recent novice who was so tall that a cassock long enough could not be found to fit him.

Concerts were organised in Boho and Derrygonnelly and a sale of work was organised by the Ladies' Committee, but the big event was The Graan Carnival which opened on 2 April. A tent which could accommodate up to a 1000 people was procured and erected in a field close to the main road not far from The Graan. Goal-posts were erected in a nearby field and a football tournament was organised in which seven teams took part. The carnival continued for eighteen days with different functions in the marquee – dances, whist-drives, ceilidhes and fashion parades; children's sports were organised on the second Sunday with a drill display, a fancy dress parade and a novelty football match. The energetic chairman of the Men's Committee was Frank Nugent. The winners of the football tournament were Derrygonnelly Harps, beating a spirited Lisnaskea Emmet's side in a dour battle on their way to the final to take the trophy. Due to political unrest the carnival was not held in 1957, but it was revived again in 1958, and it proved a popular event in succeeding years and a valuable source of income. Fr Hubert, the Vicar, and Felix Fox, the new chairman, were instrumental in making the carnival the resounding success that it was. Ceilidhes, concerts, and dances were organised throughout the '60s culminating in the first ever Graan Dinner Dance which was held in the Maghery Hotel, Bundoran on

Graan benefactors, Rose Hynes, Agnes Cassidy and Veronica Cassidy with Frs Sylvester, Eustace and Fergus

19 April 1966. In subsequent years the Dinner Dance was held at different venues including the Imperial Hotel, Enniskillen, the Ortine, Lisnaskea, the Hillgrove, Monaghan, and the Killyhevlin Hotel, Enniskillen.

Portora and The Graan

Relations between the Protestant community and the Passionists at The Graan – which had always been good – continued to improve during this period. Novices made regular use of the outdoor swimming and diving facilities at Portora on most Thursday afternoons during the summer. Dr Rogers, the Headmaster of Portora Royal School and his wife, Mary, came to dinner at The Graan in July 1967 and a few days later the Rector was invited to give a lecture to the senior boys at Portora. On that occasion both parties enjoyed the story of how, in the early days of the Passionists at The Graan, the boys from Portora had painted the Rector's donkey red, white and blue. On hearing of the incident the Headmaster had insisted that the culprits should march to The Graan and apologise individually to the Rector. This they did and were completely disarmed when the Rector greeted them cordially, graciously accepted their apologies and then treated them to strawberries and cream.

Renovations and Changes

Renovations were being continually carried out at The Graan. The congregation was ever-increasing and it was difficult to find parking space on Sunday mornings and accommodation within the church for the crowds who attended Mass. The access road was widened and improved in 1964, the area around the cemetery laid out in gently sloping lawns a few years later and a major reconstruction of the sanctuary area undertaken in 1966 in accordance with the new decrees of Vatican II. Michael Donnelly of Enniskillen drew up the plans for the sanctuary and the work was completed in early July 1967. Not all these changes were to the liking of the 'old-timers' and one which was mentioned was the use of guitars as accompaniment for hymns set to modern tunes. It was reported that the novices seemed to relish the idea of swinging 'this banal instrument' over their shoulders and plucking its strings like trail-weary cowpokes – still, if they wanted to roll their eyes and swivel their hips, it was their prerogative; they would get arthritis soon enough!

Frs Fergus, Dermot and Conleth enjoy a joke on the occasion of Fr Dermot's Silver Jubilee of Ordination, 13 April 1967

Fire at The Graan

Fire was always a hazard at The Graan and the Enniskillen Fire Brigade had to deal with an outbreak on 14 August 1971 when the hay in a silo pit was accidentally set on fire. A much more serious outbreak occurred on 21 March 1973 when a hundred bales of hay were destroyed and a silo pit damaged. Fires followed on three successive nights with a hayshed and its contents being destroyed, an unoccupied caretaker's house damaged and an attempt made to start a fire in a confession box and the gallery of St Gabriel's Church. Six separate fires in all were dealt with and a considerable amount of damage was caused. The community was at a loss to know who had started the fire but eventually the culprit was brought to light – one of the postulants in the monastery, who was harbouring a grudge against the Novice Master for a recent rebuke. A happy sequel to these unfortunate events took place on 31 October the following year when the many local people who had helped with the rebuilding of the farmyard were entertained along with their partners to a dinner dance at The Graan – 84 people in all.

The Graan in the '70s

On 21 May 1972, Bishop Eugene O'Callaghan died in Monaghan. He had been a great friend to The Graan throughout the years of his episcopacy and the good relations nurtured by him continued under his successor, Bishop Mulligan. The Graan played an increasingly important role in the religious life of the diocese: for example twenty priests including Dean Flanagan, the Parish Priest of Enniskillen, spent a day of recollection and meditation there on 19 March 1974. Throughout the decade The Graan was used as a venue for one-day retreats for the diocesan clergy, the Pioneers, the Legion of Mary and pupils and teachers from secondary schools in the county. The good relations with Portora were also maintained, with Fr Michael Doogan, the Vicar, giving a series of lectures on the Catholic Church to senior pupils there.

The well-beloved land steward at The Graan, Eugene Mohan, died on 6 April 1971. He was well known and respected throughout the county and among the congregation at his funeral were many Protestant friends who had come to pay their respects, including the Grahams, next-door neighbours to The Graan, and faithful friends of Eugene.

On 22 August of the same year (1971) Fr Alexis Boyd, a former Rector of The Graan, died in the County Hospital, Enniskillen, after a long illness. He was a noted preacher, a great missioner and a much-in-demand confessor. Bishop Mulligan and Dean Flanagan attended his Requiem Mass and 157 mourners were subsequently entertained to lunch and refreshments provided by a hard pressed Rose Gilmurray and Brother Benedict Sheridan.

Eugene Mohan

Some of the Religious who attended the Mission and Retreat Meeting at The Graan, 25-27 November 1980. Fr Aidan Troy, the Provincial, is 5th from the left in the front row

The Lourdes Grotto (Courtesy of Pat Lunny)

The Calvary at The Graan (Courtesy of Pat Lunny)

Stained glass windows in The Graan church (Courtesy of Pat Lunny)

The church interior (Courtesy of Pat Lunny)

Prayer room at The Graan (Courtesy of Pat Lunny)

The shop (Courtesy of Pat Lunny)

Praying for Fermanagh

Altar servers with Fr Brian D'Arcy

The Passionist Community at The Graan lost another great stalwart on 11 January 1974 with the death of Fr Stephen Lafferty, a native of Irvinestown, who had

Fr Stephen Lafferty

celebrated his Golden Jubilee just a year previously. In his youth he had been a pupil of De Valera and had received a congratulatory telegram from him on the occasion of his Jubilee. Fr Lafferty had spent twelve years ministering to the Australian Province. He had been Rector in The Graan from 1956-1959. Two others who were closely associated with The Graan died during the '70s – Fr Felim Kelly on 19 June 1973 and Fr Malachy Geoghegan on 18 April 1975. Both of them regarded The Graan as their spiritual home.

Fund raising for The Graan and the Passionist Foreign Missions continued throughout the 1970s. Fr Dermot Patrick (Hilarion) Cleary distinguished himself as a function organiser and fund raiser *extraordinaire*. In 1973, a dinner dance and raffle were held once again in the Maghery Hotel. First prize in the raffle was a Volkswagen car and the event raised £9,000 – a far cry from the modest sum of £110 raised at a similar function some seven years earlier. In June 1975, a charity football match took place in Lisnaskea in aid of The Graan Building Fund. The teams in contention were Jimmy Magee's 'All-Stars' and the Fermanagh's Junior All Ireland Champion's team of 1959. The main organisers were Jim Bartley and Sean McGrade. In 1983 a similar match took place between the 'All-Stars of Yesteryear' and Jimmy Magee's 'All-Stars of Radio and TV', with a youthful Fr Brian D'Arcy lining out for the latter team, and two postulants for the opposing team. The spirit of fraternal friendship was strained but not broken and The Graan received £800 from the event.

By 1975, it was becoming obvious that due to the ever-increasing numbers attending The Graan something would have to be done to enlarge the car park, regulate the flow of traffic and either build a new church or extend the existing one. An extension was eventually decided upon and work began the following year. It was completed by November 1977 and the dedication ceremony took place on the 20th of that month, with Bishop Edward Daly, a native of Belleek, and Bishop Mulligan of Clogher present. The addition of a north and south transept almost doubled the seating capacity, virtually giving us the church we know today. Thousands attended the ceremony and two marquees were erected to cater for the overflow where the congregation was able to follow proceedings on closed-circuit television. The extension cost approximately £100,000, and a dress dance in the Gresham Hotel, Dublin, on 18 February went some way in allaying the expense.

Workmen at The Graan, 1976

(L – R) Fr Ignatius Waters, (Rector), Mr Noel McAree, architect, Messrs Hartness and Robinson, quantity surveyors, Brother Paul McKeon, clerk of works, Messrs Joseph and Ignatius Conway, main contractors, Mr Thomas McCaffrey, foreman, and Fr Dermot P (Hilarion) Cleary, (Vicar/Bursar).

PASSIONIST FATHERS DEVELOPMENT FUND
for
THE GRAAN, ENNISKILLEN, CO. FERMANAGH
SECOND ANNUAL

DRESS DANCE

at the

Gresham Hotel, Dublin

on

Friday, 18th February, 1977

9 p.m. — 2 a.m.

* SPOTS AND OTHER NOVELTIES *

PROCEEDS IN AID OF THE GRAAN CHURCH BUILDING FUND

DINNER 9 p.m. sharp.   TICKET £10.00

*Gresham Hotel offers Special Reduced Terms for Patrons
of above for Overnight or Week-end Stay.*

Telephone (01) 746881   № 343

Re-dedication Mass after extension to St Gabriel's Church, 20 November 1977

The carpark was also reordered; the new front lawns were levelled and footpaths and steps from the carpark laid; the steward's house was renovated and a ring road was provided, which made access and egress much easier for the large numbers attending services. A new porch was also built at the front of the monastery. Brother Paul took a leading part in these renovations and he was ably assisted by John Dooris, 'Dando' Simpson, Leo Hoy, Vincent Convey and Johnny Cadden.

In 1976 the novitiate moved from The Graan to Crossgar, bringing to an end a whole era in The Graan's history.

Towards the New Millennium

Bishop Mulligan retired in 1979 and was replaced by Bishop Joseph Duffy who had been a curate in Enniskillen parish. He knew The Graan well and was well-disposed towards the Passionist Community. He was a frequent visitor to The Graan and held many of the diocesan conferences there. In May 1983, Monsignor Cahill, the Parish Priest of Enniskillen, invited the Passionists at The Graan to give their first ever mission in the parish. They brought in all their available big guns for the occasion, with Frs Salvian Maguire, Pat Duffy and John Friel as preachers, and a visitation team of Frs Denis and Andrew and Brothers Denis,

Eugene and Angelo. In August 1986 the Clogher Diocesan Assembly met at Dromantine and during their absence the Passionists looked after a large section of the diocese, with Frs Germanus and Evangelist taking up residence in the Parochial House, Enniskillen and Fr Charles going to Clones.

Fund raising as ever was a problem and, with the decision in February 1982 to renovate the choir and church confessionals at a cost of £35,000, the usual strategies were put into action. Fr Brian D'Arcy, then Superior of Mount Argus, using his showbiz contacts, organised a concert in the Killyhevlin Hotel, at which Susan McCann was the main attraction, and a show in the Ritz Cinema, Enniskillen, at which the Clipper Carlton Showband featured. It was not the first and it would not be the last occasion on which the world of show business generously offered their services to The Graan to help relieve the burden of debt which costly renovations had entailed.

Tommy and Dolly Moohan on their Wedding Day at The Graan, 1936

Tommy and Dolly Moohan celebrate their Golden Jubilee at The Graan with Fr Germanus in 1986

Death at The Graan

On 3 March 1985, The Graan suffered the worst tragedy in its history. Sergeant Hugh McCormac of the RUC had just got out of his car to attend 10.30 Mass and sing in the choir, when he was shot dead by an IRA gunman. Sergeant McCormac had been accompanied by his wife, Anne, and their three children, Elaine, David and Darren, all of whom were unharmed. Brother Mark O'Reilly, who had been inside the monastery, ran outside to help the family when he heard the shots. The dreadful deed greatly upset the community and was strongly condemned in a press release by Fr Aidan Troy, the Provincial Superior of the Passionists, in the course of which he wrote:

For nearly one hundred years, The Graan has been a place of refuge for peoples of all creeds, all denominations, all political persuasions. We have made many sacrifices to ensure that all people would find a forgiving, welcoming

*God when they came to The Graan …
This murder has horrified and
sickened all who come to our Church.
We condemn the murder in the
strongest possible way. We offer our
sympathy to Sergeant McCormac's
wife and to his family'.*

healing apostolate at The Graan, with
people coming from far and near to be
blessed by him. A shy, kindly, friendly
man, in 1985 he published a popular book
of poems called *Gleanings from The Graan*.
He died on 9 March 1988 and is buried in
the cemetery adjoining The Graan.

Wedding of David McCormac and Ursula Mullin at The Graan, 17 June 2008

In June 2008 Sergeant McCormac's son, David, married his bride, Ursula Mullin, in St Gabriel's Church, The Graan, leaving the McCormac family with a truly joyous memory of The Graan.

Two other deaths which greatly saddened the community were those of Fr William Hickey and Fr Arthur Kerrigan. Fr William was born in Co Mayo in 1912, professed at The Graan on 4 November 1934 and ordained six years later. He is best remembered in Fermanagh for his

Fr Arthur (Francis) Kerrigan was born in Belfast in 1913. He was professed in 1933 and ordained in 1939. He spent a few years in Scotland before coming to the Graan where he remained for over forty years. He had remarkable healing powers and he dedicated his life to the old and the sick, for whom he had great compassion; he was renowned for his special blessing for which people travelled from all over Ireland. Fr Arthur became a familiar figure in the

Fermanagh countryside, riding around on his bicycle visiting people and blessing them. He even cured their sick animals! Widely loved and respected, he died in the Erne Hospital on 4 December 1989. He is buried at The Graan.

Fr Arthur Kerrigan

Recent Years at The Graan

At the time that Fr Brian D'Arcy arrived as Superior, in December 1989, it was becoming obvious that major changes would need to take place at The Graan. In a sermon on 8 December 1991, Fr Brian outlined his reasons for the changes: as training for young Passionists was being centralised in Dublin, The Graan was no longer needed as a novitiate; there was no longer need for a fifty-room building since it was unlikely that the Community there would number more than ten in the near future. At the same time, Fr D'Arcy

assured the people that the Passionists were *not* selling the farm, were *not* selling the monastery and were *not* leaving The Graan. The 150-acre farm would be advertised for leasing, thus providing a steady income and lessening the dependence on weekly collections. The existing monastery was to be leased as a nursing home and replaced by a new, smaller, purpose-built monastery, which would be functional, easier to run and more suited to the needs of a modern monastic Community. Plans went ahead and the community moved into the new building at the end of December 1992. The Graan Abbey Private Nursing Home, with which the Passionist Community at The Graan has a close working relationship, opened its doors a few weeks earlier. A new era had dawned and all the commitments which Fr D'Arcy had given the loyal supporters of The Graan had been fully honoured. The Community at that time consisted of Frs Brian, Evangelist, Jerome, Gary and Victor and Brother Mark.

There has always been a close relationship between The Graan and the Mercy Sisters in Enniskillen. Through the years priests from The Graan gave countless retreats to the Sisters. It was fitting then that when the farmhouse at The Graan became available in 1993 Mercy Sisters came to live there and to work closely with The Graan Community. They do so to this very day.

The Graan today (Courtesy of Pat Lunny)

There was widespread and genuine sadness throughout the whole community on the death of Fr Jerome Maguire on 16 June 2002. He was a Fermanagh man, a native of Springfield,

Fr Jerome Maguire

and was regarded as a father figure by all who knew him. He was the first member of the Passionist Congregation to be waked in the new Graan Monastery and his passing left a huge gap in the Passionist Community at The Graan.

Fr Dermot Patrick (Hilarion) Cleary

Another Fermanagh man, Fr Dermot Patrick (Hilarion) Cleary, died on 22 June 2005. He had been Vice-Rector and Bursar in The Graan between 1974 and 1980. From 1983 to 1992 he was in charge of PAM, the group collecting money for the Overseas Mission of the Province. In 1992 he became chaplain to the Gardaí and was stationed at Mount Argus. He is remembered in Fermanagh as an outstanding preacher and for his enthusiastic and innovative fund-raising campaigns for his beloved St Gabriel's.

A Golden Jubilee

Fr Marius Donnelly celebrated the Golden Jubilee of his ordination in May 2002. As is fitting, there were numerous celebrations. Marius invited his family and friends to a Mass in the Prayer Room at The Graan. Close on eighty people attended, including Monsignor Sean Cahill. Fr Brian preached at the Mass and the Graan Community hosted a reception for all the guests in the new restaurant in Bellanaleck, which was run by John Donnelly, a nephew of Fr Marius. Next day Marius preached at the main Masses in the church, thus helping the local community to celebrate his Jubilee too.

The Last Decade

The first years of the new millennium have seen the small band of Passionists at The Graan consolidate their position in the lives and affections of the people of Fermanagh and surrounding counties. Prayer groups meet on weeknights and a young adults' group – later renamed *'Anam Cara'* – meets once a month on Saturday afternoons. The ever popular Novena of Hope attracts huge crowds and eminent speakers like Peter Quinn, former President of the GAA; Sean Boylan, Jarlath Burns and Mickey Harte from the same Association; Archdeacon Pringle of Rossorry; and the Passionists' own experienced team of preachers.

Celebrities from the media and the world of showbusiness and many other famous and not so famous people also come along to tell their story and share, with a rapt congregation, their own experience of life. The Graan Dinner Dance with its draw continues to be an important date in the social calendar and, together with The Graan Lottery, is an important fund-raiser. There have been highlights, too, during the decade – the altar servers visit to Croke Park, *Anam Cara's* outing to Glendalough, Fr Brian's preaching engagement in Rossorry Parish Church and the annual Harvest Thanksgiving Festival, with all the food and gifts distributed by the St Vincent de Paul Society to deserving poor in the locality. Despite his many commitments and obligations, Fr D'Arcy's prodigious literary output continues with *Reflections from the Heart, A Little Bit of Hope,* an autobiography – *a Different journey* – and most recently, *Through the Year.* There has been sadness, too, with the death of Fr Tom Devitt and the sudden and unexpected deaths of Fr Oswald and Fr Michael Doogan, which left the Community at The Graan devastated and the wider community of the Passionists bereft of three dearly loved, widely respected and affectionately remembered members of the Congregation.

Fr Michael Doogan (1943 – 2008)

Fr Michael Doogan had been a member of the Community at The Graan since 2004. He had been vicar at The Graan earlier in his career. His grandfather came from Derrylin, but Michael was born in Glasgow on 18 December 1943. His niece, Jane, works in Afghanistan as a diplomat. At the age of twenty Fr Michael joined the Passionists, entering the novitiate at The Graan in September 1963. After ordination on 19 December 1970 he spent some years preaching missions and retreats all over Ireland and Scotland. He came to The Graan in the early 1970s. Subsequently, he was Rector and Parish Priest in Holy Cross, Ardoyne, and St Mungo's, Glasgow. He also served in Crossgar and in Paris before coming back to The Graan. As well as being a gentle and compassionate confessor, Fr Michael was a gifted singer and musician. He loved playing the organ for liturgical celebrations and his piano playing got countless parties off to a rousing start.

The Community in The Graan at present consists of Fr Brian D'Arcy (Rector), Fr Anthony O'Leary (Bursar), Fr Marius Donnelly, Brother Mark O'Reilly, Fr Myles Kavanagh and Fr Ailbe Delaney. Throughout the 100 years of its existence,

The Graan has been a nursery for vocations for those wishing to pursue a religious life, and the following are among those from the locality who were influenced to join the Passionists: Fr Eustace McCauley, Fr Celestine Whiteside, Fr Stephen Lafferty, Fr Alexis Boyd, Fr Jerome Maguire, Fr Valentine McMurray, Fr Finian Harte, Fr Livinius Owens, Fr Angelo Boylan, Br Bernard McManus, Br Brendan Cassidy, Fr Columb O'Donnell, Fr Salvian Maguire, Frs Marius and Cosmas Donnelly, Br Mark O'Reilly, Br Paul McKeon, Fr Sylvius McGaughey, Fr Dermot Patrick (Hilarion) Cleary, Br Oliver Dolan, Br Norbert McPartlin, Br Vincent McCaughey, Fr Arthur McCann, Fr Brian D'Arcy, Fr Gary Donegan.

Tuesday Night Prayer Group at The Lourdes Grotto

Banner of Our Lady of Holy Hope

The above banner was brought to England by Blessed Dominic Barberi (1792 - 1849). It was he who brought the Passionists to England in 1842. In England, the banner was used in processions in honour of Our Blessed Lady. The banner seems to have been kept in the novitiate in Aston Hall, Staffordshire, and later in Broadway, England.

In 1908 the novitiate moved to St Paul's Retreat, Mount Argus, Dublin, and the following year it moved to St Gabriel's Retreat, The Graan, Enniskillen. The novices brought with them the Banner of Our Lady of Hope. Each day, in the afternoon, after Vespers and meditation, the novices recited the Rosary in procession through the novitiate corridors, or, in fine weather, in the garden. At the head of the procession, the Banner of Our Lady of Holy Hope was carried by a novice.

After restoration, the banner is now in the 150th Year Exhibition of the Passionists in Ireland in Mount Argus Church, Dublin.

Blessing of Peace Garden in memory of St Charles

Anam Cara at Mass Rock in Achill

Altar servers on day out to Croke Park

Anam Cara Prayer Group on a night out in Donegal

The Graan staff, February 2009

New altar servers, 2004

Fr Brian and Archdeacon Cecil Pringle (Courtesy of 'The Fermanagh Herald')

Christy Kenneally and Fr Brian at Novena of Hope (Courtesy of 'The Fermanagh Herald')

*Patsy Treacy, Mickey Harte (Tyrone Gaelic Football manager) and Fr Brian D'Arcy at Novena of Hope
(Courtesy of 'The Fermanagh Herald')*

Fr Victor Donnelly, a former member of The Graan Community

Passionists at The Graan 2009

Fr Anthony O'Leary

Fr Ailbe Delaney

Fr Marius Donnelly

Fr Myles Kavanagh

Brother Mark O'Reilly

RECTORS OF THE GRAAN

1909-1911	Revd Fr Eugene Nevin
1911-1914	Revd Fr Eugene Nevin
1914-1917	Revd Fr Francis Kelly
1917-1920	Revd Fr William Brennan
1920-1923	Revd Fr Gerald O'Boyle
1923-1926	Revd Fr Gerald O'Boyle Revd Fr Brendan Keegan
1926-1929	*Division of St Joseph's Province* Revd Fr Kieran Farrelly (Oct 1926)
1929-1932	Revd Fr Kieran Farrelly
1932-1935	Revd Fr Alexis Boyd
1935-1938	Revd Fr Alexis Boyd
1938-1941	Revd Fr Sylvius Rudden
1941-1944	Revd Fr Terence Barrett
1944-1947	Revd Fr Terence Barrett
1947-1950	Revd Fr Placid McLoughlin
1950-1953	Revd Fr Alphonsus McGlone
1953-1956	Revd Fr Alphonsus McGlone
1956-1959	Revd Fr Stephen Lafferty
1959-1962	Revd Fr Anselm Keleghan
1962-1965	Revd Fr Fergus Loughrey
1965-1968	Revd Fr Dermot Power
1968-1971	Revd Fr Damian Wilson
1971-1974	Revd Fr Flannan McNulty
1974-1977	Revd Fr Ignatius Waters
1977	Revd Fr Flavian Kinna
1978-1980	Revd Fr Fabian Grogan
1980-1983	Revd Fr Germanus McGrinder
1983-1986	Revd Fr Germanus McGrinder
1986-1989	Revd Fr Patrick Duffy
1989-1992	Revd Fr Brian D'Arcy
1992-1996	Revd Fr Brian D'Arcy
1996-2000	Revd Fr Charles Cross
2000-2004	Revd Fr Brian D'Arcy
2004-2008	Revd Fr Brian D'Arcy
2008-	Revd Fr Brian D'Arcy

Fr Brian D'Arcy, the current Superior of The Graan, is one of Ireland's best known and best loved priests. He is a native of Bellanaleck, who entered The Graan in 1962 and was ordained by Bishop O'Callaghan in St Michael's College, Enniskillen, in 1969. He celebrated his first Mass at The Graan on 21 December 1969. An accomplished author, newspaper columnist, broadcaster, journalist and chaplain to the entertainment industry, he is the first priest in Ireland to be admitted to the National Union of Journalists. He served as editor of *The Cross* magazine, production editor of the Catholic Communications Centre in Dublin, Parish Priest of Mount Argus and Superior in Crossgar before returning to The Graan as Superior. His memoir, 'a Different journey', reached number 1 in Ireland, selling over 50,000 copies. He has been nominated to receive an honorary doctorate from the University of Ulster this summer for services to the promotion of religious understanding.

The Graan Centenary Prayer

1909 - 2009

O Lord we thank you for the many blessings you have given to your people here at St Gabriel's, The Graan.
As we reflect on a centenary of service we realise that your generosity knows no limits.
You have healed us with gifts of compassion, reconciliation, unity and hope.
You have raised us up through the prayers, preaching and listening ear of countless Passionists.
You have taught us that when we share your Passion, you always walk with us.
Whether we know it or not you, our loving God, are always by our side in the good and bad times of our lives.
We thank you for the Passionists, many people, workers, helpers and generous benefactors who have kept the memory of your Passion alive since 1909.
We ask your forgiveness for the hurts we've caused, intentionally or unintentionally. As we look back with gratitude may your Holy Spirit guide us to whatever future awaits us.
Help us to celebrate in a joyous, holy way this centenary year.
May The Graan always be a place of peace and prayer for the rich and poor; for those who believe and those who walk in darkness; for the sick and for the healthy; for the lonely and for the lost.
And may the Passion of Our Lord Jesus Christ be ever in our hearts and on our lips,

Amen.

Our Lady of Hope pray for us. St Gabriel pray for us.